World At Risk

CLIMATE CHANGE

Andrew Solway

FRANKLIN WATTS
LONDON•SYDNEY

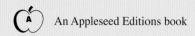
An Appleseed Editions book

First published in 2009 by Franklin Watts

Franklin Watts
338 Euston Road, London NW1 3BH

Franklin Watts Australia
Level 17/207 Kent St, Sydney, NSW 2000

© 2009 Appleseed Editions

Appleseed Editions Ltd
Well House, Friars Hill, Guestling, East Sussex TN35 4ET

Created by Q2AMedia
Editor: Geoff Barker
Art Director: Rahul Dhiman
Designer: Harleen Mehta, Ritu Chopra
Picture Researcher: Dimple Bhorwal, Shreya Sharma
Line Artist: Sibi N. Devasia
Colouring Artist: Aadil Ahmad
Technical Artists: Abhideep Jha, Bibin Jose, Manoj Joshi

ISBN 978 0 7496 8811 0

Dewey classification: 363.738'74

All words in **bold** can be found in Glossary on pages 42–43.

A CIP catalogue for this book is available from the British Library.

Picture credits
t=top b=bottom c=centre l=left r=right
Cover Images: Shutterstock: bg, Inset: Rita Januskevicik/Shutterstock:cl, Robert Adrian Hillman/Shutterstock: c, Shutterstock: cr

Andrejs Pidjass/Shutterstock: 3, Morane/Fotolia: 9, NOAA: 11, Science Photolibrary/Photolibrary: 12, Mattias Malmer: 15,
EvansArtsPhotography/iStockphoto: 17, Agmit/iStockphoto: 18, Rajesh Kumar Singh/Associated Press: 19, Ashley Cooper/Corbis: 20,
Enote/iStockphoto: 21, Gergana Todorchovska/123RF: 22, Nancy Nehring/iStockphoto: 23, Jill White/Fotolia: 24, Bigstockphoto: 25,
James Gathany/Centers for Disease Control: 26, Touhig Sion/Corbis Sygma: 27, NOAA: 30:, Associated Press: 31, Noel Kemp/
Photo Researcher/ Photolibrary: 32, Randy Montoya/Sandia National Laboratories: 33, Photomo/Dreamstime: 34, Ashley Cooper/
Corbis: 35, American Honda Motor Co. Inc.: 36, Associated Press: 37, Vincent Yu/Associated Press: 38,
Johannes Compaan/Shutterstock: 39m, Lorenzo Mondo/Shutterstock: 39tl, EvansArtsPhotography/iStockphoto: 43.
Q2AMedia Art Bank: 8, 10, 13, 14, 16, 28, 29.

Printed in China

Franklin Watts is a division of Hachette Children's Books,
an Hachette UK company.
www.hachette.co.uk

CONTENTS

1

HOT, HOT, HOT!

Recent years have seen heatwaves scorch the globe, from Australia to North America. Temperatures soared as Europe wilted under a record heatwave in summer 2003.

Too hot for comfort

In almost every European country, the **heatwave** in 2003 caused enormous problems. In southern Europe there was a drought that lasted longer than the heatwave itself. Farm crops across southern Europe were poor because of this. In eastern Europe drought and high temperatures also affected the crops. In the Ukraine and Moldova, nearly three-quarters of the wheat harvest was lost.

The highest temperatures of all hit Portugal. In Amareleja, in south-east Portugal, the temperature reached 48°C on 1 August. The very hot, dry weather led to many forest fires and 10 per cent of Portugal's forests were destroyed.

Earth Data

- According to **data** from NASA (National Aeronautics and Space Administration), the eight warmest years on record have all occurred since 1998. The 14 warmest years on record have all occurred since 1990. 2005 was the warmest year on record globally, with 2007 and 1998 equal second warmest.

During the 2003 heatwave, many people enjoyed a sandy 'beach' by the River Seine. But elsewhere in Paris, the heat was killing people.

Temperature (°C)

0   10   20   30   40   50

This map shows just how hot the USA was on 20 July 2006. Dark orange areas on the map were over 40°C.

Source: NOAA (National Oceanic and Atmospheric Administration)

The human cost

The biggest cost of the heatwave was in human lives. Thousands of people died, many of them as a result of heat exhaustion combined with dehydration (water loss). Normal body temperature is 37°C. When the surrounding temperature is hotter than this, the body cools down by sweating. Sweating removes water and salt from the body, which need to be replaced. If they are not, the body eventually stops sweating, and the **core temperature** of the body begins to climb. Eventually heat exhaustion can result in death. The old, the young and people who are already ill are the most vulnerable.

In France, high temperatures in northern regions had disastrous results. Many people in this area were not used to the heat and did not drink enough water. As a result thousands died, most of them old people or young children. Across the whole of Europe, 35,000 people are estimated to have died because of the 2003 heatwave, and 13,000 of these deaths occurred in France.

Worldwide changes

The European heatwave was not an isolated event – this is only one example that illustrates the pattern of worldwide changes in the **climate**. For example, in India in 2003 nearly 1,700 people died as temperatures soared to over 47°C in the southern state of Andhra Pradesh. Three years later, in 2006, there was a heatwave across the USA and Canada in July and August. Temperatures reached 54°C on one farm in South Dakota. At least 330 people died due to the effects of the North American heatwave, including as many as 31 deaths in New York City and over 160 in California alone. There was also another heatwave across Europe in 2006, and during the following year a heatwave affected South Asia, Russia and China.

This change in climate affects the whole world. Heatwaves and **droughts** are becoming more common, but the changes also include increases in floods and storms. Taken together, the overall pattern of these extreme weather events seems clear – our planet is getting warmer.

9

Scientific studies

Scientists have been finding evidence of **climate change** for over 30 years. They have also investigated the causes of climate change. For many years these causes were not clear. Some scientists believed the changes were part of large weather cycles lasting thousands of years, perhaps related to changes in the activity of the Sun. However, over time evidence grew to show that the changes in climate are the result of human activities.

The Intergovernmental Panel on Climate Change (**IPCC**) is an international group of scientists based in Switzerland that was set up in 1990 to draw together all the scientific research being carried out into climate change. In its third report on Climate Change in 2001, the IPCC reported increases in worldwide air and ocean temperatures, widespread melting of snow and ice, and rises in sea level. By the fourth IPCC report in 2007, understanding of the effects of human activity on the climate had greatly improved. The Panel was over 90 per cent certain that human activities have caused the climate to get warmer, and the vast majority of scientists agree with their findings.

Over the last 150 years, the average global temperature has gradually risen. This graph shows that, year by year, the temperature varies quite widely. However, over the whole period, the trend is clearly upwards.

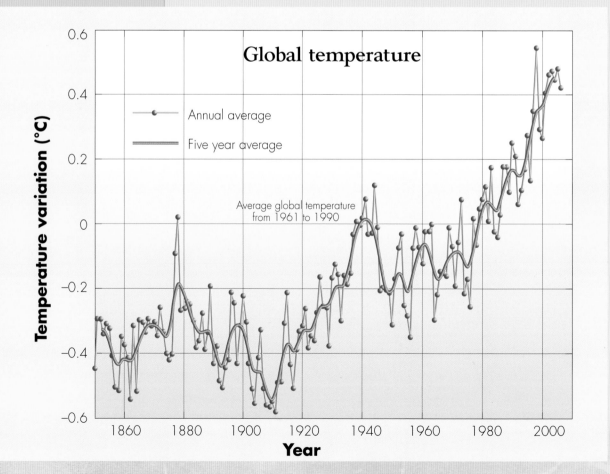

Hurricane Katrina hit New Orleans, USA, in 2005. It destroyed the city's flood defences and made millions homeless. Experts predict that climate change will lead to further powerful hurricanes like Katrina.

Future changes

The IPCC's 2007 report also predicts that the climate will continue to warm in the future. From changes that have happened in recent years, it is already clear that the climate is warming faster than in the past. Using **computer models** (see page 17), the IPCC estimates that the average temperature worldwide will rise by between 1.1°C and 6.4°C during this century. Even the lowest prediction is nearly twice as big as the temperature increase over the last 100 years. By 2100, unusually hot periods like the summer of 2003 in Europe will not be exceptional – they will actually be the norm.

World at risk

In the past 150 years, changes to the **atmosphere** have affected the climate. The whole world is at risk from these changes. What is causing climate change? What effects are we seeing now? And what are future effects likely to be? This book will look at these questions, and at what we can be done now.

PLANET WATCH

» Scientists at the IPCC say that temperature rises of more than 2°C above **pre-industrial** levels would be disastrous for people and wildlife. Even a rise of 2°C will bring big problems.

» Temperatures have risen by 0.76°C since 1900.

» Over the last 50 years, temperatures have risen nearly twice as fast as over the last 100 years.

2

EVIDENCE OF CLIMATE CHANGE

Scientists noticed climate changes in the 1930s. People thought these changes were part of a natural cycle, but it emerged that human actions might be responsible.

Earth Data

- For long periods in the past, the climate was much warmer than it is today. The average temperature on Earth today is around 15°C. From about 250 million years ago to 50 million years ago, average global temperatures were around 22°C.

- The last Ice Age ended roughly 14,000 years ago.

Looking into the records

The first place to look for evidence of climate change is past weather records. The oldest continuous weather records are from central England – they date back 300 years or more. But it is only in the last 150 years or so that weather measurements have been made using similar methods and instruments. This makes it possible to compare weather records. Combining the results of the different weather records gives a very variable temperature graph (see page 13), but the overall trend is clearly upwards.

Scientists examining an **ice core** in Antarctica. Ice cores can give us valuable information about the climate in the past.

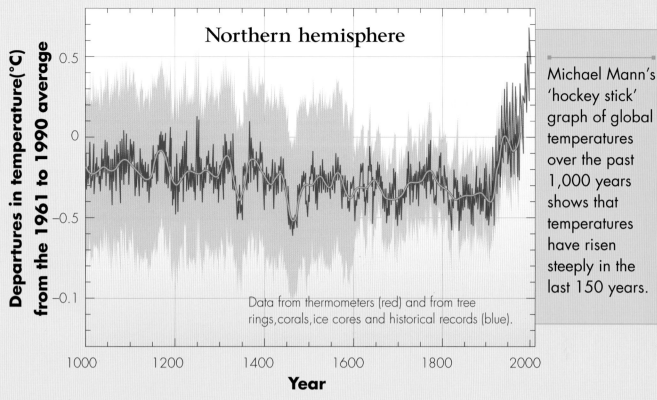

Northern hemisphere

Departures in temperature(°C) from the 1961 to 1990 average

0.5
0
−0.5
−0.1

Data from thermometers (red) and from tree rings, corals, ice cores and historical records (blue).

1000   1200   1400   1600   1800   2000

Year

Michael Mann's 'hockey stick' graph of global temperatures over the past 1,000 years shows that temperatures have risen steeply in the last 150 years.

Weather variations

Weather records dating from the past one and a half centuries are not sufficient to be sure that there is anything unusual in the changes that have happened to climate. Researchers knew from other written evidence that, for instance, there was a long period of warm weather in Europe from about the 10th to the 14th centuries. Documents also show that between 1550 and 1850 there was a period known as the 'Little Ice Age', which brought bitterly cold winters to northern Europe. At first, people assumed that the rise in temperatures we have seen in the last 50 years was just part of a natural variation in climate that happens every few hundred years.

Rings, cores and sediments

To find out about the climate further back in time, scientists carefully examined **tree rings** and samples in ice from the North and South poles, as well as **sediments** from the ocean bed. Each of these different sources shows traces of how the world's climate has varied from year to year. Tree rings, for example, can provide clues about climate in the past few thousand years. Ice cores go back even further in time. They can give us information on what the weather was like several hundred thousand years ago. Sea sediments, however, can provide data on temperatures of the oceans millions of years ago.

Putting it all together

By the 1990s, scientists and **meteorologists** had thousands of records from these different sources. The American **climatologist** Michael Mann put together many weather records from different parts of the world and from different periods of time. He used **statistical methods** to combine all the information into a graph of average global temperatures for the last 1,000 years. The graph (above) showed that average global temperatures stayed more or less constant until about 150 years ago. At this point the temperatures started to rise. It was the clearest evidence yet of climate change.

What is causing climate change?

The evidence that exists from temperature records shows that global temperatures began to rise about 150 years ago. So what caused this rise?

The explanation for the main cause of climate change was first suggested in 1896 by a Swedish chemist called Svante Arrhenius. He suggested that the carbon dioxide gas that was released into the atmosphere by the burning of coal and other fuels could cause the Earth to become warmer.

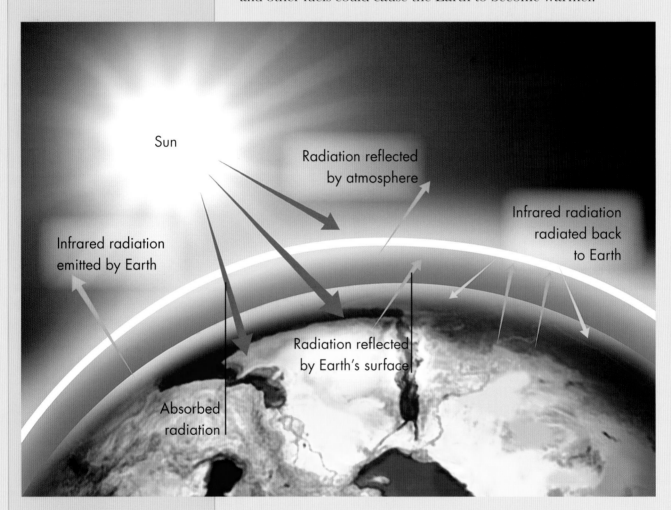

Sun

Radiation reflected by atmosphere

Infrared radiation radiated back to Earth

Infrared radiation emitted by Earth

Radiation reflected by Earth's surface

Absorbed radiation

The greenhouse effect: how gases in the atmosphere help to warm the Earth.

The greenhouse effect

Carbon dioxide affects the global temperature through something called the greenhouse effect. The glass in a greenhouse lets in sunlight, which warms the inside. However, the glass does not let the heat out so easily. So in sunny weather, the inside of a greenhouse is warmer than its surroundings.

The Earth's atmosphere is a bit like the glass in a greenhouse. It helps to stop heat from the Sun from escaping into space.

Greenhouse gases

Carbon dioxide in the atmosphere acts as a **greenhouse gas**. This means that it absorbs heat **radiation**, and so prevents some heat from being lost into space. This keeps the Earth much warmer than it would be without an atmosphere. The average surface temperature over the whole of the Earth is about 15°C. The Moon, which has no atmosphere and no greenhouse effect, has an average surface temperature of −18°C.

The greenhouse effect is not in itself a bad thing. In fact, it is essential to life. Without it, the Earth would be too cold for living things to survive. However, the extra carbon dioxide that humans have pumped into the atmosphere has tipped the scales. Now the Earth is getting too hot for comfort.

Other greenhouse gases

Carbon dioxide is not the only greenhouse gas. Two other gases produced by human actions are **methane** (natural gas) and nitrous oxide. Methane is produced from landfill sites, coal mining and farming. Nitrous oxide is produced mainly from agriculture, when bacteria in the soil break down artificial **fertilisers**.

PLANET WATCH

» There are 200 times less methane and 1,200 times less nitrous oxide released into the atmosphere than carbon dioxide. However, these greenhouse gases have a much stronger effect than carbon dioxide. Even in these small amounts they cause about 12 per cent of the total greenhouse effect.

The thick atmosphere of Venus is rich in carbon dioxide. Because of the greenhouse effect, the average surface temperature on Venus is 464°C.

Carbon emissions

People have influenced the greenhouse effect. From the 1850s, humans began burning coal, and later oil and gas, in enormous quantities. Burning **fossil fuels** releases a huge amount of carbon dioxide into the atmosphere. Since the mid-1970s, 157 billion tonnes of carbon dioxide have been produced by human activities, and **carbon emissions** are rising at a rate of around 2.5 per cent every year.

Levels going up

Carbon dioxide levels have risen for several reasons. First, the world population has grown enormously. In 1850 it was about 1.2 billion. Today it is nearly six times this figure and still rising. Second, we use far more energy per person today. This is partly because most people in more economically developed countries (**MEDCs**) have cars, central heating, electric lighting and many other devices that use energy. Large amounts of energy are also used in producing food and in making goods. As countries develop a better standard of living, the amount of energy they use rises rapidly. This is happening today in many less economically developed countries (**LEDCs**), such as China, India and South Korea.

It was suggested in 1896 that carbon dioxide might be causing climate change, but it took years to gather evidence that it was actually happening. The Earth's atmosphere, and the changes in it that produce weather patterns, is extremely complicated. This has made it hard to prove the connection between carbon dioxide levels and climate change. However, scientists are now convinced that increases in atmospheric carbon dioxide are the main cause of climate change.

CO_2 levels in the atmosphere
Average monthly figures measured at Mauna Loa, Hawaii

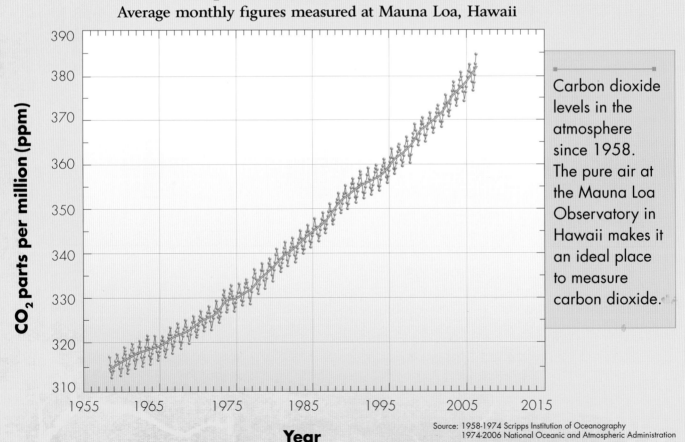

Carbon dioxide levels in the atmosphere since 1958. The pure air at the Mauna Loa Observatory in Hawaii makes it an ideal place to measure carbon dioxide.

Source: 1958-1974 Scripps Institution of Oceanography
1974-2006 National Oceanic and Atmospheric Administration

Factories like this one produce carbon dioxide and other emissions that add to the greenhouse effect.

Computer models

Some of the most powerful tools used by scientists and meteorologists in climate change research are called computer models. A computer model is a **mathematical simulation** on a computer of a real-life object, event or series of events. For example, an aircraft simulator includes a computer model of the cockpit of an aircraft which can mimic the behaviour of an aircraft in flight.

On the same basis, scientists have used computers to build models of the Earth's atmosphere. They first test the model on previous major changes in the climate. As scientists have managed to learn more and collect more information, they have been able to improve their computer models. In this way they can more accurately reflect what climate change happened in the past, and they can use the same models to predict what might happen in the future.

PLANET WATCH

» In 1850, carbon dioxide concentration in the atmosphere was around 280 parts per million (ppm). Since then carbon dioxide levels have risen to nearly 390 ppm.

» Until 2005, the USA had the highest carbon dioxide emissions in the world.

» In 2006, China became the largest carbon dioxide producer. China's carbon dioxide emissions are rising by 11 per cent each year.

17

3

EFFECTS ON LAND AND SEA

The world is getting warmer, but in January 2008 global temperatures were lower than in previous years. Is climate change really happening?

Climate varies naturally

The weather can vary an enormous amount from year to year, or even within a year. This variation can all be natural. However, over a period of years it is possible to notice changes in the climate, despite natural variations.

There will be cooler years as well as warmer years. As climate change continues there will be fewer and fewer cooler years though. Overall, temperatures will continue to rise.

The summer of 2007 was the wettest ever recorded in the UK. Heavy rains caused flooding in several parts of the country. Climate change could lead to more flooding like this.

Warmer poles

The effects of climate change vary from place to place around the world. For example, during the last 20 or 30 years, temperature measurements have shown that the Arctic region has warmed more than twice as quickly as other parts of the world. Generally, the **tropics** are warming less than the areas around the North and South poles.

Droughts and floods

As well as differences in warming, the changes in climate are also having an influence on the amount of rain that falls. Some areas are already receiving more rainfall. Extremely heavy rains caused floods across South Asia in 2007. Twenty million people were affected by the floods, and over 250 people were killed. IPCC predictions suggest that by 2050 there will be more winter rain and snow in most northern regions.

In contrast to regions that are becoming more prone to flooding, other areas of the world are already receiving much less rainfall than before. For example, between the years 2003 and 2008, large regions of Australia suffered from a sustained drought, the worst in 1,000 years. The IPCC predict that by 2050 there will be less rain in Australia and Central America, as well as southern Africa.

Extreme weather

A change that is already affecting the world and is likely to get worse is that, as the climate warms, there are more extremes of weather. In the 1950s, on average every year there were around 200 extreme weather events, such as droughts, floods, heatwaves, storms and wildfires. In recent years, the average number of extreme weather events has risen to almost 1,600 per year – an increase of about 800 per cent.

2007 saw three periods of flooding across India and Bangladesh. About 1.5 million people were made homeless by the flooding.

A rising tide

As the world's climate continues to get warmer, the height of the oceans and seas is rising. Pacific island groups such as Tuvalu and Vanuatu (see map) are suffering floods several times every year. In Vanuatu some villages have already moved to higher ground to escape the flooding. People from Tuvalu may soon have to abandon their island home altogether.

Warming and melting

Two main effects cause the ocean levels to rise as the climate gets warmer. The first of these is called ocean expansion. As the sea begins to get warmer, it expands slightly, taking up more space. This expansion causes a rise in sea levels. Ocean warming is responsible for just over half of the global rise in sea levels since 1993.

The second cause of sea level rise is the melting of polar ice-caps and **glaciers**. The ice-cap on the Antarctic is the largest store of ice on Earth. Other ice areas include the Greenland ice-cap and glaciers in many mountain ranges

All these ice areas are melting. Worldwide, snow and ice cover is decreasing by 1–3 per cent every 10 years. The Greenland ice-cap and the Arctic ice sheet are melting especially fast. Since 1970, 9 per cent of the Arctic ice sheet has melted every 10 years.

The low-lying islands of Tuvalu in the South Pacific ocean suffer regular floods because of rising sea levels.

Map of South Pacific Islands, Australia and New Zealand

Arctic summer melt

Changes in the Arctic ice sheet are especially worrying. Large parts of the Arctic Ocean are covered by ice. Some of the ice remains from year to year, and some melts each summer and freezes again in winter. In recent years, more and more permanent ice has melted each summer. According to recent research from the National Center for Atmospheric Research (NCAR) in the USA, the Arctic Ocean could be ice-free in summer by 2040.

Effects of sea rises

As sea levels rise, more low-lying coasts and islands will flood. If sea levels continue to rise, some areas will disappear underwater. If the sea rises by 1 metre, nearly the whole of Bangladesh, a country of 150 million people, will flood.

Climate change has led to faster melting of icebergs, especially in the Antarctic. One unexpected effect is that there has been an explosion of wildlife around the icebergs, because the meltwater is rich in minerals.

PLANET WATCH

» According to the IPCC 2007 report, the sea could rise between 9 and 88 cm by 2100.

» Researchers in Australia have shown that between 1870 and 2004, sea levels climbed by 20 cm. Levels rose faster in the last 50 years of this period.

Changes in farming

As the climate changes, it affects the kinds of plants that can grow in an area. This is beginning to transform farming. In some areas, such as northern Europe and North America, computer models predict that the climate will become warmer and wetter, which could improve the yields of farm crops. In other places, land will become less productive. According to the 2007 IPCC report, in some African countries the amount of food produced from crops could be halved by 2020.

Adapting to change

In all areas, as climate changes increase, farmers will need to adapt what they grow and how they grow it. Farmers in cooler regions will begin to grow crops that are currently grown in the Mediterranean or in Florida. For farmers in warmer areas, **irrigation** will become critical. As the recent drought in Australia showed (see page 23), reduced rainfall means there is less water for farm crops. The farmers who are likely to suffer most from climate change are those in the poorest areas. Most of the poorest nations in the world, such as Ethiopia, Malawi and Niger, are in tropical Africa, where decreases in rainfall are predicted to cause a reduction in **crop yield**.

A field of sunflowers in southern France. Crops like sunflowers will soon grow in northern Europe if climate change continues to warm the planet.

Peach potato aphids are common pests of potatoes in the UK and USA. As the planet warms, populations of such insects are likely to grow as they breed for longer each year.

If climate change happened gradually, farmers would have time to adapt their crops to new growing conditions. However, most recent evidence suggests that climate change is happening even faster than anticipated. This could be disastrous for agriculture everywhere. The weather will be unpredictable, and many more crops will fail because they cannot survive the weather conditions.

Pest invasion

As the climate gets warmer, conditions improve for many of the **pests** that destroy farm crops. At present, in many farming areas pests die off or become dormant in winter, then numbers increase in spring. In the past 15 years pests such as **aphids** have begun breeding earlier in the year. At some point, winters will become warm enough for most insects to survive, and pest numbers could rise enormously. Insect numbers are already rising in some places. In Alaska, for example, since 1988 there have been large increases in spruce bark beetles, which have affected over 5 million acres of forest. Such pest outbreaks are almost certainly due to climate change.

PLANET WATCH

» In 2005 one in six countries suffered food shortages because of drought.

» In 2003 Australia produced large amounts of food for **export**. From 2003 to 2008, the country suffered an extended drought.

» During the Australian drought, rice production fell by 98 per cent. Cotton production dropped by 66 per cent and wheat production by 61 per cent.

» In April 2008, rice prices rose by 50 per cent in two weeks, partly due to the fall in Australian rice production.

23

4 EFFECTS ON WILDLIFE

Wildlife and wild habitats are affected by local changes in the climate. The more slowly the climate changes, the more chance wildlife will have to adapt.

Changes in the Arctic

The fastest changes in the climate are taking place in the Arctic. The Arctic is home to a wide variety of wildlife, including polar bears, Arctic foxes, seals and walruses. All these animals rely on the sea ice that forms in the Arctic Ocean each winter. The sea ice connects the Arctic pack ice to surrounding land areas such as Canada and Russia. It provides wildlife with places to feed and to bring up their young. The ice is also an important migration route for caribou and musk ox.

The warming planet means that more sea ice melts in the Arctic each summer. Polar bears are good swimmers, but they need some sea ice to survive.

Some studies suggest that in future the Amazon rainforest could look like this savannah landscape.

Meltdown

As the climate continues to warm, the sea ice melts earlier and re-forms later each year. This is affecting all Arctic species. To look at one example, polar bears rely on sea ice as a platform for hunting seals and other wildlife. In summer, the bears move to land areas, where they survive on very little food. If the sea ice is late forming in the autumn, the bears begin to starve. Also, females raise cubs on the sea ice during the winter. If the sea ice lasts for less time, the cubs cannot develop and grow properly.

It is predicted that all the Arctic ice could melt each summer as early as the year 2040. If this happens, polar bears and other species will not have enough time each year to get food and raise young. Many scientists think that polar bears will die out before the end of the century.

Drier rainforests

Rainforest areas are slowly becoming drier as the climate changes. This is beginning to affect the wildlife in areas such as the cloud forests of Costa Rica. These mountain forests rely for moisture on low clouds, which form close to the ground and soak the ground and the vegetation with water. Since the 1990s, drier weather has meant that the clouds have been forming higher up, and some parts of the cloud forest are not getting enough water.

One animal that may already have died out is the golden toad. This small, orange-yellow toad was quite common in the cloud forests until the 1990s. However, the drier climate has meant that the pools that the toads rely on for breeding have dried up. No golden toads have been seen since 1991, and the species is feared to be extinct.

Spreading disease

Climate change is likely to have direct effects on human health. One obvious cause of health problems is the increase in events such as floods, droughts and hurricanes. People die in floods and hurricanes, but such extreme weather events also mean an increase in unclean water. This in turn causes diseases such as **diarrhoea**, cholera and liver infections. Droughts cause food shortages, which can lead to **malnutrition**. Such disasters can also leave large numbers of people without food and shelter.

Insect infections

Another major health problem caused by climate change is the spread of infectious diseases to new areas. Many infectious diseases are spread by insects. Malaria, for example, is a disease caused by a **microbe** that lives in the **salivary gland** of some female mosquitoes. When a malaria-infected mosquito bites a human, it injects the microbe into the blood, and the person gets the disease.

Malaria is spreading

Malaria is a disease that at present only occurs in tropical countries. However, even small changes in temperature can allow mosquitoes, ticks and other insects that carry diseases to spread to new areas. According to scientists at the London School of Hygiene and Tropical Medicine, cases of malaria are now being found in mountain areas in Africa, where malaria has never been seen before. Insects have also carried malaria and other diseases to higher regions in Colombia in South America, and Nepal and New Guinea in Asia. Temperature rises have caused glaciers to melt, leaving areas of higher ground bare. These areas have then been **colonised** by plants. Once the plants are established, mosquitoes and other insects can **migrate** upwards to higher altitudes, bringing disease with them.

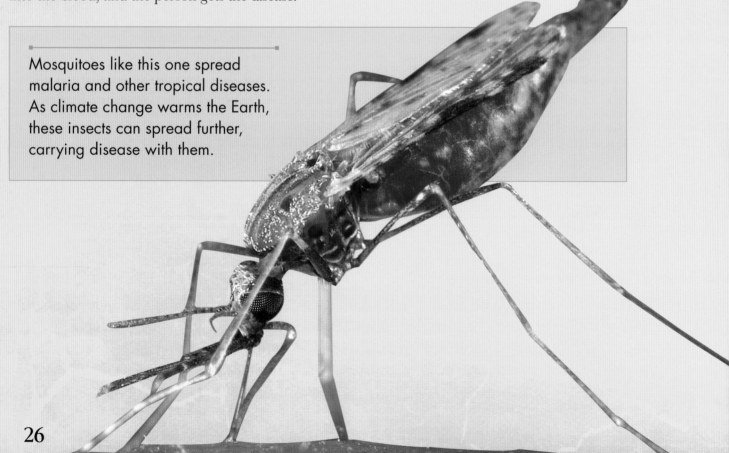

Mosquitoes like this one spread malaria and other tropical diseases. As climate change warms the Earth, these insects can spread further, carrying disease with them.

Insecticide is sprayed in city streets in New York, to try and kill mosquitoes carrying West Nile virus. Before 1999, the disease was found only in Africa.

West Nile virus

In the past 20 years, several tropical diseases have spread north through the USA and Canada. West Nile **virus** is a mosquito-borne disease, which comes originally from Uganda, Africa. In 1999 the disease was somehow carried to the USA, and there was an outbreak in New York. Most people who caught the disease were only mildly ill, but some suffered from a much more serious form of the disease which can be fatal. Birds spread West Nile virus across North America. Since 1999 there have been thousands of cases of the virus, and some deaths.

Bluetongue

The spread of tropical diseases to cooler climates affects farm animals as well as humans. Bluetongue is a disease carried by a tiny midge found in tropical Africa and South America. The disease infects sheep and some other grazing animals. Since 2006 there have been bluetongue outbreaks across Europe, killing around 70 per cent of the animals that become infected.

PLANET WATCH

» In 2000 the World Health Organization (WHO) estimated that climate change was responsible for 2.4 per cent of worldwide diarrhoea, and as much as 6 per cent of malaria in some nations.

» Before 2001 there were only 149 cases of West Nile virus in the USA, 18 of which were fatal. Between 2002 and 2006 there were 23,818 cases, 941 of which were fatal.

5

NO QUICK SOLUTIONS

Greenhouse gases have greatly changed the air and oceans. These changes will affect the climate for many years to come and may take centuries to reverse.

Heating the oceans

Water has a very high heat capacity. This means two things. First it takes a lot of heat to warm up a litre of water to a particular temperature, compared to warming up the same volume of another material, such as rock. Second, water takes longer to cool down than other materials, because it absorbs more heat. The oceans contain a huge volume of water. It takes far more heat to warm them up than it takes to warm the land. The oceans have absorbed more than 80 per cent of all the heat added to the climate system. The oceans are so vast that all this extra heat has only warmed them slightly. Scientists can measure the temperature of the oceans worldwide, and at different depths, using Argo floats (see right).

Map of the oceans' acidity

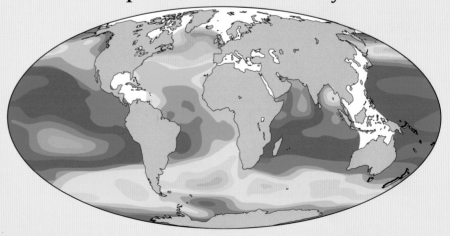

Amount below normal sea surface pH

-0.12   -0.1   -0.08   -0.06   -0.04   -0.02

Normal sea pH (around 8)

More acidic

Earth Data

- The atmosphere contains roughly 750 billion tonnes of carbon dioxide. The oceans hold about 50 times this amount.

- Between 1800 and 1994, the ocean removed 118 billion tonnes of carbon dioxide from the atmosphere.

- A study by the US National Center for Atmospheric Research (NCAR) in 2005 predicted that, even if greenhouse gas levels were held steady at the levels in 2000, it would still take 100 years for the climate to stop warming.

This map shows changes in acidity of the ocean surface caused by the absorption of carbon dioxide. Orange areas are most acidic, while white areas have normal sea pH (about 8).

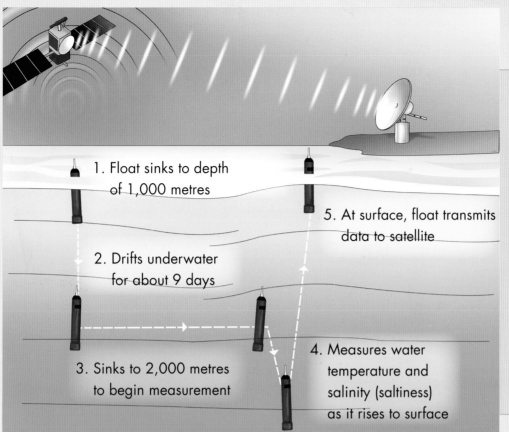

1. Float sinks to depth of 1,000 metres

2. Drifts underwater for about 9 days

3. Sinks to 2,000 metres to begin measurement

4. Measures water temperature and salinity (saltiness) as it rises to surface

5. At surface, float transmits data to satellite

Just how warm are the seas? Over 3,000 special Argo floats measure the oceans' temperature. The floats sink and drift to a depth of 2,000 metres. They record temperatures as they rise to the water surface, then transmit the data they have collected to a satellite.

Slow to cool down

Once they have warmed up, the oceans take a long time to cool down again. This effect is called 'thermal inertia'. If you cook food in the oven, then turn the power source off, the food will continue to cook in the oven, because the heat stored in the oven walls will continue to heat the air inside it. In a similar way, thermal inertia means that, even if we manage to prevent greenhouse gas levels from rising any more from today, climate change will continue to happen. This is because the heat already stored in the oceans will continue to warm the air.

Easy to absorb

As well as absorbing heat from the Sun, the oceans are able to absorb carbon dioxide gas from the atmosphere. Chemical exchanges of carbon dioxide between the water in the seas and oceans and the Earth's atmosphere have helped to stop atmospheric carbon dioxide concentrations from rising too quickly.

Carbon dioxide gas dissolves easily in water. As levels of carbon dioxide in the atmosphere rise, more carbon dioxide dissolves in the oceans. A certain amount of carbon dioxide is also taken up by microscopic, plant-like creatures called **phytoplankton**. If animals eat the phytoplankton, the carbon dioxide that the plant-like creatures absorbed is released back into the air. However, some of the **plankton** die and sink deeper into the water, where the carbon dioxide may stay for many years. About 48 per cent of all the carbon dioxide that humans have ever produced has ended up in the oceans.

Now absorbing less

Research by an international team of renowned scientists has found that the oceans are actually absorbing less carbon dioxide now than in the past. Between 1995 and 2005, the oceans' ability to absorb carbon dioxide halved. Carbon dioxide that is not absorbed in the oceans remains in the atmosphere – and adds to global warming.

Acid seas

When carbon dioxide dissolves in water, it forms a weak acid called carbonic acid. So as more carbon dioxide dissolves in the oceans, the water becomes more acidic. So far, the extra carbon dioxide that the oceans have absorbed has only changed ocean acidity slightly. As we keep producing more carbon dioxide, however, oceans will become more acidic.

Carbon dioxide is not absorbed evenly over the whole ocean (see map, page 28). In some areas more carbon dioxide is absorbed, making the water more acidic. Two examples are the northern Atlantic Ocean and parts of the northern Pacific. These oceans are closer to industrial areas where more carbon dioxide is produced. The water is also cold, and colder water can absorb more carbon dioxide.

Studies carried out all over the world show that more acidic seawater affects ocean life. Corals, certain kinds of mollusc and some species of plankton rely on materials from the water to make their chalky shells. When the water is more acidic, there is less chalky material in the water, so shell-making becomes more difficult. The result is that the animals grow more slowly.

Ice on the seabed

By absorbing heat and carbon dioxide, the oceans have greatly reduced the effects of climate change. However, substances buried at the bottom of the ocean could reverse all these benefits and push the planet into a burst of rapid global warming. The sediments of the ocean floor contain large amounts of a substance called 'methane ice'. This looks like ice, but is actually a frozen mixture of water and methane (natural gas). One litre of the ice contains, on average, about 168 litres of methane.

Climate change is affecting the acidity of the oceans. As the sea gets more acidic, it becomes harder for shellfish such as this pteropod, or sea butterfly, to make its shell. The pteropod from the Gulf of Alaska is an important food source for fish such as salmon and cod.

The film *The Day After Tomorrow* imagines what could happen if the Gulf Stream stops. The film exaggerates, but if the Gulf Stream did stop, parts of Europe and North America would be much colder.

» The Gulf Stream is a warm ocean current that starts in the Gulf of Mexico and influences the climate of the eastern coast of North America. It also brings milder weather to northern Europe. As the ocean warms, computer models suggest that melting of ice in the Arctic could slow down or even stop the Gulf Stream. This would have the strange effect of making the climate in northern Europe and in parts of North America much colder. Some recent research has shown evidence that the Gulf Stream is slowing down. However, even if results are correct, it will take over 200 years for the Gulf Stream to stop.

A methane 'burp'

If the oceans warmed enough, the methane ice in the ocean floor could melt and release huge quantities of methane gas. It is estimated that the oceans contain between 500 and 2,500 billion tonnes of methane ice. (For comparison, the atmosphere contains 700 billion tonnes of carbon dioxide.) Methane is a far stronger greenhouse gas than carbon dioxide. This methane 'burp' could cause a huge **spike** in global warming.

But will a methane 'burp' happen? Few scientists think that a methane 'burp' is likely today. Even if methane is released, this will happen over thousands of years rather than all at once.

6 WHAT CAN WE DO ?

Soon the Earth could become too hot for humans to survive. If we want to address the problem of climate change, we need to cut carbon dioxide emissions drastically.

Making drastic cuts

Temperatures have risen by 0.76°C since 1900. Scientists at the IPCC believe that a temperature rise of more than 2°C above pre-industrial levels will be catastrophic for us and our world. To stop global temperatures from climbing more than 2°C, we need to cut carbon dioxide emissions by at least 60 per cent by 2050. Some scientists believe we need to make carbon dioxide emissions cuts of up to 80 per cent.

Earth Data

Researchers are experimenting with new ways of generating electricity without using fossil fuels. These include:

- Electricity from rain: raindrops falling on a pressure-sensitive surface can produce an electric voltage.

- Electric paint: a paint that produces electricity in sunlight.

- Electric bacteria: bacteria that can produce electricity when fed on waste water.

- Electric clothing: clothes made from threads that produce electricity as they rub together.

The Itaipu Dam in South America is one of the biggest hydroelectric plants in the world. Electricity generated by water power does not produce greenhouse emissions.

At a solar thermal power station, collecting mirrors like these focus the Sun's heat on to a water-filled pipe. The water is heated to steam, which can be used to power an electric generator.

How to cut emissions?

There are two main ways to reduce emissions. The first is to cut back. Modern fossil fuel power stations have greatly reduced emissions. If all fossil fuel power stations did this, it would reduce overall carbon emissions. Some large cars produce over 300 grams of carbon dioxide per kilometre, but the most efficient small cars produce only 99 grams. If all car emissions were improved to the lowest level this would also reduce emissions. However, cutbacks are not a complete solution. In the longer term, we need to replace fossil fuels. Replacement types of energy should produce little or no carbon dioxide and should be **renewable**.

About 65 per cent of the world's electricity is made using fossil fuels. As a result, electricity generation is the largest single source of carbon emissions in most MEDCs. In the USA, electricity generation produces 40 per cent of all carbon emissions. One of the most effective ways to reduce carbon emissions would be to find ways of generating electricity that do not produce carbon dioxide.

Cleaner energy

Since people first began to realise the problems with fossil fuels, scientists have been developing ways of generating electricity that produce less carbon dioxide.

Approximately 35 per cent of the world's electricity is produced using hydroelectricity (water power) and nuclear power. Wind power, solar (Sun) energy and wave and tidal energy are other 'cleaner' methods of generating electricity that do not produce carbon dioxide. Except for nuclear power, these different **technologies** use energy sources that will not run out. Electricity production from alternative energy sources such as solar energy and wind power is growing very quickly. For example, between 1996 and 2006 the amount of electricity produced using wind power grew by almost 1,000 per cent, while solar energy grew by almost 2,000 per cent. But even with this rapid growth, wind, solar, wave and tidal energy produce only around 4 per cent of the world's electricity.

Drawbacks with new energy sources

Alternative ways of producing electricity also have drawbacks. Hydroelectric energy, for example, is clean and efficient, but most large rivers that are able to support hydroelectric plants are already being used. Nuclear power stations are very expensive to build in the first place, and the waste that they produce remains a **radioactive hazard** for hundreds of years. Solar power stations cannot work at night, and wind power is only available when the wind blows. Wave and tidal power are promising energy sources, but we do not really have the **technology** to use them as yet.

There is no single replacement

No single form of energy is ever going to be able to replace fossil fuels for electricity generation. However, a combination of a mixture of different energy types as well as a small number of fossil fuel power stations could reduce carbon dioxide emissions considerably.

Better buildings and devices

Individuals and groups of people around the world are saving energy in various ways. One of the biggest uses of energy is for running houses and other buildings. Improving the insulation of existing buildings, and cutting down on ways that warm air can escape to the outside, can greatly reduce the amount of energy needed to keep them warm in summer and cool in winter. New buildings can be designed to take advantage of sunlight and cooling breezes to keep a building at a fairly constant temperature without using either heating or air conditioning. Inside buildings we can save energy by using energy-efficient machines and devices. Low-energy light bulbs, for example, use about one-sixth of the energy of a conventional bulb. Energy-saving washing machines use a third less energy, while energy-saving fridges reduce energy use by two-thirds.

Cutting waste

Reducing waste is another way that we can reduce energy use. Producing new materials uses huge amounts of energy compared with reusing materials. Making aluminium from recycled scrap, for example, uses 95 per cent less energy than making aluminium from ore (bauxite, or rocks containing aluminium). Reducing the amount of packaging we use, and reusing or recycling waste materials, are both ways of reducing energy use.

Modern low-energy light bulbs look very similar to ordinary light bulbs, but they use about a sixth of the energy.

Bedzed is an energy-efficient group of houses and flats in London, UK. The buildings are designed to use far less energy than normal. The energy they do use (including electricity for running cars) comes from solar and other clean forms of power.

Better transport

Saving energy on transport is another way of cutting carbon emissions. Public transport uses far less energy per person than using private cars, so one way to cut down on energy use is to improve public transport systems, especially in cities. The city of Curitiba in Brazil has a very good public transport system that saves energy and reduces pollution. Buses run every 90 seconds at peak times, and special bus lanes mean that the buses avoid getting stuck behind other city traffic. Many people travel by bus instead of using cars. The result is that carbon emissions from transport in Curitiba are 30 per cent lower than cities of a similar size. If other cities made similar improvements in public transport, it would greatly reduce carbon emissions from transport.

PLANET WATCH

» An average home in Europe needs about 250 kW of power to heat each square metre of floor space. Low-energy homes built in Stuttgart, Germany, need only 12.8 kW per square metre. This is a saving of nearly 95 per cent.

» The most fuel-efficient car in the world is the PAC-Car II from Switzerland. This super-light one-seater can travel 5,385 km on 1 litre of petrol. Despite its fuel efficiency, the car is not in general production as it was built simply as a test car.

35

The Honda FCX is an experimental car that uses fuel cells. These fuel cells are powered by hydrogen, and the only emissions are of water vapour.

Reducing fuel use

Improving the efficiency of cars and other vehicles is another way to reduce energy use. Car engines have become far more efficient in the last 25 years. However, at the same time they have become heavier and more powerful, so these improvements have not led to reduced **fuel consumption**. As a result, the overall **fuel economy** of cars has actually got worse since 1987, when on average cars used less fuel than today. Manufacturers need to save weight on cars and use smaller engines.

New engine designs

A promising new kind of engine being developed at the Massachusetts Institute of Technology is one that produces nearly twice the power of a normal engine of the same size, but with the fuel consumption of a small engine. This kind of technology could help us to build cars that use far less fuel in the future.

A great deal of careful scientific research has gone into making vehicle engines that do not use fossil fuels. Hybrid vehicles have both a normal engine and an electric motor. They are the most fuel-efficient cars on the road, but they are about 12 per cent more expensive to buy.

Electric cars

Electric motors are more efficient than conventional engines, and the vehicles themselves produce no carbon emissions. However, fossil fuels such as coal, oil and gas continue to produce the majority of our electricity, so charging up the battery produces carbon emissions. A few commercial electric cars are available now, but they are more expensive than conventional cars.

A new way of thinking

To make a real difference to carbon dioxide emissions, however, we need to think in a new way that brings together all kinds of ideas about energy saving and new forms of energy. For example, if we design cities so that people live close to where they work, this would reduce carbon emissions because people would travel less. Well-designed buildings, heating schemes for whole districts rather than individual houses, and cheap and efficient public transport are other ideas that could really help to reduce our over-reliance on fossil fuels.

Carbon capture

One possible way to reduce carbon dioxide in the air would be to 'capture' carbon dioxide and somehow lock it away. Capturing carbon dioxide can be done by '**scrubbers**' that remove it from exhaust gases. The carbon dioxide can then be stored either in the ground or deep in the oceans.

All the different stages of carbon capture and storage are feasible, but at present no power stations are using the whole system. A report by the IPCC says that by the year 2100, carbon capture and storage could account for 15 to 55 per cent of the total carbon dioxide reductions that we need to make.

PLANET WATCH

» One way that has been proposed for capturing carbon dioxide is to add large amounts of iron to the oceans. Iron encourages the growth of plant-like phytoplankton. Adding iron to the ocean would produce a burst of growth in phytoplankton, which would take up carbon dioxide from the air. However, much more research is needed before this method can be used safely on a large scale.

The Japanese E200 is the world's first hybrid train. It uses a combination of a battery-powered motor and a diesel engine to cut carbon emissions by 60 per cent.

Climate change is here

For many years climate change was a subject for fierce debate. Some scientists and **conservationists** were convinced that climate change was caused by human activities, while others wanted more proof that the changes in the climate were not part of a natural cycle. Today most scientists agree that climate change is happening, and that the main cause is the amount of carbon dioxide that we have pumped into the atmosphere.

Taking action now

The scientific arguments have convinced most politicians, and the governments of many countries are taking action to reduce their carbon dioxide emissions. There is also progress on an international level. In 1992 the UN (United Nations) held the first Conference on Environment and Development. One of the main purposes of the Conference was to take action to slow climate change. Targets for reducing carbon emissions by 2012 were agreed by a group of countries, in a document called the Kyoto Protocol. Unfortunately, it took many years for most countries to make a firm commitment to the Kyoto Protocol, and it seems likely that many nations will not meet their Kyoto targets.

Slow progress

Much more needs to be done if we want to avoid environmental disaster. The message from the scientific world is that we need to reduce carbon dioxide emissions by at least 60 per cent – maybe 80 per cent – by the year 2050. If climate change does not slow down, millions or even billions of people may die, as temperatures soar and floods and drought become widespread. Governments may have passed laws to reduce carbon dioxide production, but overall the world's carbon emissions continue to climb, and any progress in emissions reduction is painfully slow.

An Inconvenient Truth is a film about how we are causing climate change and the dangers it holds. The star of the film is politician Al Gore, who was once Vice President of the USA. The film was a huge success and won two Oscars.

If we want to maintain a healthy balance of life on Earth, we need to address the problem of climate change sooner rather than later. That means acting now for the benefit of future generations.

A dangerous experiment

There are still many arguments over climate change. Some people maintain that we cannot prove that human activity is the cause. Others agree that climate change is caused by humans, but believe that people will not accept changes to their lives that will reduce carbon emissions. Meanwhile, we continue to carry out a dangerous experiment. We are loading the atmosphere with more and more carbon dioxide. We cannot afford to carry on pumping greenhouse gases into the atmosphere without worrying about the consequences. If we do not act immediately, it may just be too late.

PLANET WATCH

» Initially 55 countries signed the Kyoto Protocol on climate change. The treaty was agreed in Kyoto, Japan, in 1997, but did not come into force until 2005. One notable absence was the United States of America. Overall, nations agreed to reduce their carbon dioxide emissions by 5 per cent by 2012. Each country agreed to separate targets for their emissions. MEDCs agreed to cuts in their emissions, but some countries with low emissions were allowed to increase them. As of May 2008, 182 countries had signed and ratified the Protocol.

FACTS AND RECORDS

Top ten carbon dioxide (CO_2) producers

Rank	Nation	Annual emissions (tonnes)	
		2007	**2005**
1	China	1,801,931	1,514,127
2	USA	1,586,213	1,576,536
3	Russia	432,486	410,290
4	India	429,601	382,739
5	Japan	337,363	335,707
6	Germany	209,624	213,970
7	Canada	144,738	146,704
8	United Kingdom	144,726	149,132
9	South Korea	130,072	123,421
10	Italy	129,855	123,246

(Source: Preliminary 2006/7 Global and National Estimates by Extrapolation - from Carbon Dioxide Information Analysis Center (CDIAC))

This table shows the top carbon dioxide emitting countries in the world in 2007. The USA was previously the biggest emitter, but now it is China. Countries such as China and India have far bigger populations than the USA. As these nations become more industrialised, their carbon emissions will continue to grow.

Rank	Nation	CO_2 (tonnes per head)
1	Qatar	16.73
2	Kuwait	10.39
3	United Arab Emirates	7.50
4	Bahrain	7.41
5	Trinidad and Tobago	6.83
6	Luxembourg	6.75
7	Aruba	6.26
8	USA	5.32
9	Falkland Islands (Malvinas)	4.96
10	Australia	4.95

This table shows the countries with the highest carbon emissions per person. The highest emitters are mostly small countries. If these countries reduced their carbon emissions, it would have very little impact on world carbon emissions, because the populations are so small.

IPCC climate change predictions

IPCC predictions of future climate change have been calculated for a number of different scenarios. Each scenario is a different 'storyline' of how the world might change between now and 2100.

A1   The world economy grows rapidly and world population reaches a peak around 2050. New, more efficient technologies are introduced quickly.

A2   The world is more fragmented, with different regions growing at different rates. Overall economic growth is slower than in other scenarios. The population increases continuously until 2100.

B1   Population growth is similar to that in A1, but economies become less about making and selling things and more about supplying services and information. Clean and efficient energy technology is introduced.

B2   Local and regional communities make great efforts on climate change problems. Population growth is continuous but slower than in A2. There is an emphasis on **sustainable** solutions to problems.

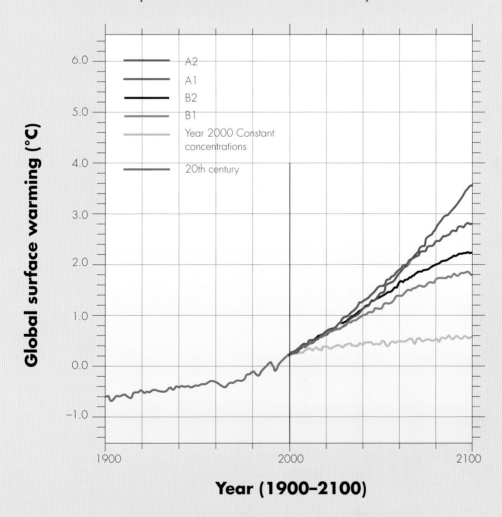

GLOSSARY

aphid
small insect which feeds on plants, damaging crops

atmosphere
the air around the Earth

carbon emissions
gases containing carbon, released when a fuel is burned, for example

climate
the average weather of a region over a period of many years

climate change
climate change usually means long-term changes in the climate that are being caused by human activities

climatologist
a scientist that studies the climate

colonise
when a plant or animal spreads into a new area

computer model
a computer program that is designed to mimic as closely as possible a process in the real world

conservationist
a scientist or other person who is working to try and conserve (keep safe) natural environments and the living things in them

core temperature
the temperature deep inside the body, which nearly always stays constant

crop yield
the amount of a crop harvested from a fixed area of land

crustacean
a group of animals that includes crabs, lobsters, shrimps and related species

data
information, often in the form of measurements or numbers

diarrhoea
a condition where the body loses water in the faeces

drought
long period with little rainfall

export
something that is sold abroad

fertiliser
substance (usually chemical) added to soil or water to increase the amount of crops it can produce

fossil fuels
a fuel derived from fossilised plant or animal remains

fuel consumption
the amount of fuel used by a vehicle to travel a fixed distance

fuel economy
the use of as little fuel as possible

glaciers
'rivers' of ice that form either high in the mountains or on ice-caps

greenhouse gas
gases in the atmosphere that absorb heat from the Sun and prevent it escaping into space

heatwave
a period of exceptionally hot weather

ice core
a long cylinder of ice obtained by drilling down deep into an ice-cap or ice sheet

IPCC
the Intergovernmental Panel on Climate Change, an international group of scientists who gather together scientific evidence on climate change and report every few years on how the climate is changing and what is likely to happen in the near future

irrigation
watering crops in places where there is not enough natural rainfall for them to grow well

LEDCs
less economically developed countries, generally the poorer countries in the world

malnutrition
the lack of proper nutrition, caused by a poorly balanced diet

mathematical simulation
using maths to mimic the behaviour of something real

MEDCs
more economically developed countries, generally industrialised nations – and the richer countries in the world

meteorologists
a scientist who tries to understand and predict the weather

methane
natural gas. Methane is found in the atmosphere in small amounts. It is a powerful greenhouse gas

microbe
a very small living thing, only visible under the microscope

migrate
when a group of animals move from one part of the world to another

pest
an insect or other animal that attacks and damages food, crops or farm animals

pH
a measure of how acidic or alkaline a solution is. The pH scale runs from 0 (very acidic) to 14 (very alkaline). pH7 is neutral and the sea surface is around pH8

phytoplankton
tiny, plant-like creatures that can make their own food

plankton
plants or animals that live in the ocean and drift with its currents

pre-industrial
before the Industrial Revolution, when there were no factories or mass production of goods

radiation
rays or waves similar to light. Heat radiation (infra-red radiation) is invisible radiation with waves that are slightly longer than those of visible light

radioactive hazard
a material that gives out radioactivity (harmful types of radiation) that can make people ill or kill them

renewable
something that can be renewed

salivary gland
a gland in the mouth that produces saliva

savannah
a mix of grassland and small trees

scrubbers
special filters that can remove polluting gases from the fumes produced by factories or power stations

sediments
finely broken pieces of rock or other material. Mud, sand and silt are all kinds of sediment

spike
a steep rise and fall on a graph

statistical methods
ways of using maths to analyse and make sense of large amounts of numerical (number) information

sustainable
describing a process that can be repeated again and again without using up natural resources

technology
the practical application of scientific ideas

tree rings
the rings you can see in the cut end of a tree trunk. The number of rings are used to calculate the age of the tree

tropics
the warm areas of the world to the north and south of the Equator

virus
a very tiny kind of microbe that causes illness. Colds and flu are common illnesses caused by viruses

FURTHER READING

- *Changing Climate: Living with the Weather* by Louise Spilsbury (Raintree, 2004)
- *National Geographic Investigates: Extreme Weather: Science Tackles Global Warming and Climate Change* by Kathleen Simpson (National Geographic Society, 2008)
- *Planet Under Pressure: Climate Change* by Mike Unwin (Heinemann, 2006)
- *Renewable Energy (Energy Essentials)* by Nigel Saunders and Steven Chapman (Raintree, 2004)
- *Weird Weather: Everything You Didn't Want to Know About Climate Change, But Probably Should Find Out* by Kate Evans (Groundwood Books, 2007)

INDEX

WEBFINDER

http://epa.gov/climatechange/kids/index.html

EPA stands for Environmental Protection Agency. Their excellent site has information on climate change plus games, animations and the 'climate detectives'

http://news.bbc.co.uk/cbbcnews/hi/specials/climate_change/default.stm

Website from the BBC Newsround programme looking in detail at climate change

www.bbc.co.uk/climate/

Learn about the evidence for climate change, the impact it is having and how the world might adapt to a warming climate

http://ec.europa.eu/energy/intelligent/library/videos_en.htm

A series of videos on things we can do to fight climate change

www.zerofootprintkids.com/kids_home.aspx

Slowing climate change is all about reducing our carbon footprint (the amount of carbon dioxide we produce). This calculator helps you to work out your personal carbon footprint